KISS
ME
DOWN
TO SIZE

December 30, 1983

All the best,

Ken Rivard

KISS ME DOWN TO SIZE

Ken Rivard

thistledown press ltd.

Copyright ©Ken Rivard, 1983

Canadian Cataloguing in Publication Data

Rivard, Ken, 1947 -
  Kiss me down to size

  Poems.
  ISBN 0-920066-70-4 (bound).   ISBN 0-920066-63-1 (pbk.)

  I. Title.
  PS8585.I93K5   C811'.54   C83-091239-8
  PR9199.3.R59K5

Book design by A.M. Forrie
Cover illustration by Dianne Bersea

Typesetting by Apex Design Graphics Ltd., Saskatoon
Set in 11 point Goudy Oldstyle

Printed and bound in Canada by
Hignell Printing Limited, Winnipeg

Thistledown Press
668 East Place
Saskatoon, Sask. S7J 2Z5

Acknowledgements

Many of the poems have appeared, in an earlier version, or have been accepted to appear in *Again, Blue Buffalo, Cross-Canada Writers' Quarterly, CV/11 Dandelion, Event, Germination, Nebula, Origins, Poems n' Things, Poetry Canada Review, Quarry, The Canadian Forum, The Didsbury Booster, The Malahat Review, Vortex, Waves, Wee Giant, Whetstone* and in the following anthologies: *Alberta Diamond Jubilee Anthology* and in *Going for Coffee* edited by Tom Wayman. Some of the poems have been broadcast on *Access Radio* in Alberta.

The author wishes to thank Paddy O'Rourke, Tom Wayman and especially Patrick Lane for, more than anything else, their solid encouragement of his writing.

The author is grateful for the financial assistance of a writing grant from Alberta Culture.

This book has been published with the assistance of the Saskatchewan Arts Board, The Canada Council, and Alberta Culture.

Table of Contents

This book is for Micheline, Annie and Melissa

Girl In The Attic Picture

every morning she soft-foots
up to the attic full of sleep
looks past her window reflection
tries her damndest to will away
artifacts at her feet.

she herself becomes a childhood
doll staring out the window
where the present is only
a footstool for her watching.

as I watch again she steps more loudly
down from the present
walks straight at me warning
to never try to restrict her to a poem.

before I can respond she struts
back to her smile
back to her dusty frame.

Looking Into My Daugher's Nightmare

running skyward in dark hair
she huffs and puffs at wind
screaming around her sleep.

at my chest her perfect cloud slingshot
flings moon at stars
hoping to spotlight each fear
hiding in sky corners.

as she rubs panic from her eyes
she asks about her sleep
needing practice
and
is there a way to empty
all those black jars
on the shelves
behind her eyes?

My Daughter's Kind Of Sleep

her four-year-old dreams don't sleep.
she reassures me that the sun too
will sleep in the tree's yellow flesh
just because I had just read her a story
about the sun being afraid of cold.

two hours later she awakes
climbs out of bed dressing herself slowly
as if going to meet a lover.

and just as suddenly
she climbs back into bed alone
but under sheets says she is ready.
how will the sun be
in the rough of its leaf blankets?
she asks half-awake.

the sun overhears
by spilling its batter
like wet wild flowers
on my daughter's bed
and very carefully hugs her
in the orange of its arms.

Humpbacks In The Sky

in the early evening whales slip
across the sky leaving sunset coals to smolder
like fingers poking at black land.

whales absorb the day's heat
from a copper lake
ignoring the creators
like a faceless photographer
in a crowd.

man who took this picture
rides on mammals' backs
saddled on the quiet of tomorrow.

as the earth squeezes those last sky drops
into its breast
whales glide to a place
where picture-takers
and sky-creatures prepare
the broken day.

Might Come Alive

pouring hot water into her teapot
she stares at family photographs.
the hot steam is not permanent.
an old calendar shows a winter scene
and she's always wearing that hat of hers
as if that winter scene
might come alive
under her roof.
I once imagined that her ceiling
was scotchtaped to her sky.
an apron is so much a part of her
she tucks it in with hands that look
thirty years younger than the rest of her.
her fireplace, like an oaken animal,
listens more at night when fed.
look
her hair
her hair is becoming more like steam
and she's still trying to re-read
ancient Christmas cards.
you know the ones,
they look like shrunken skins
from the beasts of our past.

Yesterday's Glass

one of my daughters is playing
in a pool made plastic on its own.
she is washing her chest over
and over as fists of suds
drop into concentric circles
at her knees.
can I watch? I ask.
go ahead, she says,
but do not break my white circles
or my castle will flood
like yesterday's glass of milk
on the kitchen floor.

then she arcs her back
digs thumbs into soap
as if the bar were hardened tea leaves
ready to tell us all.

can you make one of those circles
stand on its rim? I ask.
watch, she says.
before I know it
the widest circle
stands on its edge
wraps itself around my neck
and kisses me down to size.

Drumheller Girls

from their graves
dinosaur bones beckon my daughters
to sandcastle soil unearthed long ago
by history of some kind.
these bones ask
why I am there too.

stories are whispered
in a million years of make-believe.
maybe I think I'm too tall to understand.

finally, I hear the dinosaurs
inviting the girls to the hoodoos
for pinball games on bumpers of stone
and
I watch any idea I had of daughters
playing in a cemetery
about as old as any excuse
I could give for being there.

Repeat Themselves

what are you doing to all those women?
today my wife was in the backyard
looking over her shoulder
waiting for you to drag her into the house
to do what all the newspapers are saying.
be careful, she is just fisted enough
to tell you to go rape yourself to death.
even the cops are saying you do a bad job.
in the newspapers they have interviewed many
of your possible victims.
they are waiting holding your number —
1. Suzanne, 25, waitress, says:
I keep myself locked in with a gun.
I borrowed it from a friend.
I take care of my child during the day.
I don't want anything to happen.
I've had my locks changed and got bars for my windows.
2. Claire, 23, secretary, says:
I'm a very cautious person.
I never go out alone at night
never take the stairs in our building.
I stay away from parking lots, take main streets
and always keep my door locked.
3. Krysia, 35, announcer, says:
I never walk down dark streets at night.
I'm worried 'cause it's all happening during the day.
I don't like to live in fear
but there's little you can do to protect yourself.

4. Danielle, 18, sales clerk, says:
I don't go home alone, I keep my doors locked.
I don't go down alleys
but I was doing those things before.
5. Debbie, 24, nursing aide, says:
I've started locking my door.
I'm more aware of things to do.
you keep thinking it won't happen to you
but I never go out alone at night
or anything like that.
5. Henriette, 58, homemaker, says:
I live with my son so I'm not too concerned
but you can't help thinking about it.
it's just awful.
7. Rose, 30, loans officer, says:
as usual, I keep my doors and windows locked.
I don't take any dark streets at night,
people are really talking about it.

there you have it
I know
I know
the women tend to repeat themselves
but they are tired of waiting
in your lines.

Turner Valley

in the grasp of his land
leaves cup color
huddling their veins
from Rocky Mountain breathing.

Turner is really a gas station philosopher
spending days in a rocking chair
studying out-of-town licence plates.

often he points to earth torches
flaming the residue of oil men
from thirty years ago.
he laughs at those
who dug their wisdom into soil
soon discovering that his skin
was beginning to wear more often
an overcoat of November night.
he tells me his wide place in the road
needed that kind of protection.

but wait
look
he is walking away from me
to lead his residents to forget
what I pretend to know;
people here need more time
to finger count harvest flecks
in the trees that were once his.

All Wrapped Up In Pincher Creek

when we first meet
you erupt the same way
those foothills suddenly
greet the mountains.

at eighty years of age
you talk about plants
as if they're made from horizon;
your eyes are blue pools
teaching roots when to drink.

one of your sons laughs
says you're full of piss n' vinegar
but there's something else there.
as you show me your seedlings
their arteries flex at us
asking you to come closer
to feel what you're really made of.

then you talk about your boys
how they stumbled like newborn garden greens
as they skated with HOCKEY NIGHT IN CANADA
humming through their limbs on a cold night.

you laugh at the reliable
seventy-year-olds playing
sonatas in the penalty boxes
they have created out of themselves
in their very own earth
and you finally ask how I feel
about soil and mountain abruptness.
you answer your own question
with a slap on the back of my silence.

Variables of My Father's Ambition

as he legs his way into the house
necktie is loosened, jacket is flung
like leftover skins from his day.
a carefully folded newspaper is tossed
onto the living-room rug in unison with his:
what's for supper, Ethel?
as if the moon were asking the sky
for its latest menu of thunderheads.

when we eat supper, he dons his comic faces
by mocking his co-workers —
their functions are beyond their control.
he doesn't even know he's doing it
as I choke from another of his custard pies
on my face.

at night when everybody is smiling in their sleep
he wakes me for a Marx Brothers movie.
I sit on the floor between his ankles
waiting for that starting gun of laughter.

his convulsions explode from my ears
to my shoulders
to my belly
and before I know it
my father and I are one loud honk
chasing skirts around the television.

during a commercial, I see my father on a studio lot
teaching The Marx Brothers how to be funny.
the way he clarifies
yes, the way he clarifies Harpo's philosophy of bum-pinching.

when the lesson is over my father is presented
with an Academy Award — best ability for comedy instruction
and The Marx Brothers promise to do their next film with him.
right away he calls me up to the stage
gives me his award with such a hilarious look
it causes all the Oscars to step down
and applaud his performance.
even the audience files up to him
like ripples of laughter dressed just right.
the only hereness left
in the wides grin of chairs imaginable
and the endless
hopes of my father.

Reliever

he strolls in from center field.
his turn to relieve.
a man in the crowd points
to the pitcher's mound
flings out advice
but the pitcher's glove catches and quietly
drops the spectator's advice on the turf.
the man, still gesturing, reminds the reliever:
keep your fastball low
don't let your curve hang
be sure your slider . . .
and the crowd gulps down
the man and his words.

reliever trudges to the mound slowing down
as his plan picks up tempo.
he looks up at the man
pretends to nod
warms up by tossing back at his father
those two words still caught
in the webbing of his glove.

Time Has Nothing To Do

John Donne wears a baseball cap
and a poem-filled mitt.
he can't make it to first base
with a small magazine editor.

his poems are not quite there.
they simply don't add enough
to the placid way of the nineteen seventies.

Donne warns the editor
if this were the seventeen hundreds ·
the editor's head would be planted
in an open field
and
all the composure in the world
wouldn't soften the influence
of the sun's fists.

Donne receives his expected sour response
saying how times are tough
and all the arrogance he could possibly muster
couldn't arm-wrestle the sun
into thinking the way he does.

For Real Shy

on the dark of the sky dance floor
moon waltzes in a room of stars.
clouds are suitors waiting in line
with dance cards at the ready
and these applicants shuffle
clearing their throats as if
their faces were pinned to their lapels.
then the men's eyes widen with black
and with music of comet fiddlers
the suitors chase imaginary skirts
across the floor of their minds.
the only choice left for the moon
as she looks down at me with embarrassment
is to hide herself in the widest possible
hoedown of white.

The Rain Has Two Parts

rain falls on the roof like an orchestra
of tin cans.
it smacks against my window
but the glass is innocent.
I know so because of how it fingers beads of prayer.
the downpour knows no rhythm
it falls in two parts
a multitude of harmonies split in half.
it happens that way
when the ground is waiting.

my mother is calling from twenty years ago.
she asks what I'm planning to grow.
one part of her question is very dry.
the other is soaking wet with what she wants
to cultivate.

it is becoming more quiet.
the rain is getting wise.
it is now only spitting carefully,
of course clearing its throat beforehand.
it's that etiquette of sky you know.

it is almost too silent now.
drops are hobbling like a
cripple in a trance
across the ears of my voice.
there is no applause.
there is only
the bass speech of no sound.

Man With The Stick

his face is furrowed with the rubber
of dull intellectual bouncing
and a one
and a two
and a three.
even his heart thumps omniscient numbness
with a silent stick strung
across a tightrope grin
(his act is life defying).

just as he's going to fall
he uses his lumber to balance
his act involving the roar of instinct
and his heady fibres of bark.
sometimes he is the stick —
figure that out for a man who insists
on being carved from his own stone.

Of His Casual Solutions

she can't stop running between sheep standing still
on her eyelids.
she has no other way to say it.
her doctor says he knows better
even though she's tried
all of his casual solutions.

no more.
no more, she says.
tonight she'll learn to smell the clean
of her own fresh ease.

in bed she decides not to trust
the honest intentions of others
and for the first time in weeks
she finds herself walking
in the most wide-open meadow
her doctor could ever imagine.

Farm Bachelor

lives with his spinster sister
but often chats alone at the window
with the nightbreeze of his curtains.

one night he announces he's off for a stroll
down the highway but she shouldn't
wait up for him.

not a half-mile from home he lies,
he lies on the road
praying for a car
to etch him on the grey.

soon his prayers are heard very clearly
a vehicle bobs over the hill
and
swerves just in time
breaking both his legs.

in the hospital he swears at the driver
for saving his remaining days for the silence
of his night drapes.

Mantras For Sale

for six dollars a month per vehicle
transcendental meditator uses
his landlady's backyard as a used car lot.
he tells me his integrity is advertised
as being sound
his guarantees are written in nods.

for six months a year he sells cars
drifts to Vancouver Island
where he sleeps with his profits
in the ribs of a camper sold to him
by a woman who only drove it to church
in case her spiritual needs
had a preference for the outdoors.

in Spring he returns
filling his landlady's yard
with contemplated sales
and in the neon sign of his deep breathing
empties her backyard
while she smiles SOLD signs
at the elements of his truth.

Memory Tablets

during irregular Alberta sky breathing
he teaches fence posts and zoo swans
how to stay tall.

for years he sorted his solitary
by the shelves in a Calgary post office
licking the shyness of his anger
onto the backs of nobody's stamps.

before that the Saskatchewan ranch life
but from the safe distance of photo albums
there's nobody there anymore
so his prairie memory tablets seek burial
in the ground of his heart.

last time I kissed his woman hello
you'd swear his privacy
if measured vertically
could wrap itself
round the highest fence post
and you wouldn't even notice
how the sky protects his wood.

Photographer's Lens

the road is made of August.
that dozing creature squinting
through the photographer's lens
is none other than the animal inside.
it doesn't believe in its own sleep.

he is that lone green tree
refusing to allow autumn into his blood.
a hawk on a cloud tells him to dance along
with the sky full of music.

the road is a piece of his mind left open.
its gravel pretends to draw shadows.
someone forgets to shut the coffin
or zip up the forest for the winter.

Fisherman's Noon

lobsters and crabs play pitch and catch
with erratic baseballs of sun.

fisherman with hip-high ambition
stabs his arm through the heat mirror
but instead of a handful of crab
grasps fickle sand shadows.

again he tries to outdo
the curves of those water tricks
but they laugh in their glimmer
and fling their deftness past his gaze
to an outfield of sky.

October On The Level

knuckled leaves fist all those gusts
down to smother the frayed bark
of my tree trunk
as if I were daring the wind
to breathe me dry.

only blades of grass know any better.
they coax me to sway
with the warm tune
plucked on sun strings:
ride the wind
not as a stubborn oak
but like saplings daydreaming
the onslaught aside.

Gull Lake Alphabet

seagulls know when dinner is served.
they drag their shadows over my campsite.
shadows are fat
gulls are not
shadows are fat.

campfire has its own alphabet.
it is teaching me how to read a man
who tells stories about generator trips to South America.
I wonder about gull habits in Lima and Peru.

to my left is an inflated silver cigar
on my right a red and white tin box with windows.
I love the water and absurdity of this place
in the above order of course.

on the road back the morning levels the sky.
to the west a giant Japanese woman is
watching over mountain and bird.
she is holding her grey fan
like a book of too many stories.
she is reading aloud to me
by asking if I like her hair
curled just the way it is.

Allowing The Moles

when I look at you
I try to realize
all those who make attempts
at following the contours of your silence
as if it will make things better.

I see them all slowly reaching beneath
rubbing you straight
across their compass readings.

but when you spoke today
you said you see them all as moles
and you want to allow them access
to the tunnels
to the tunnels of
to the tunnels of your absolute breathing
where they can live
in the dream
you are dreaming.

Ever Took Me Seriously As A C.P.R. Cop

1.
during my training
sergeant major asks what I would do
if someone starts shooting at me.
I reply: DUCK.
he says: NO, you should get down on one knee like this
and he lowers himself behind his desk
his right index finger like a pistol.
then he says: POW, POW, POW
leave as little target as possible.
POW, POW, POW? I ask.
yes, don't forget POW, POW, POW, he says.
I tell myself to remember
to always have a desk
following me around
on my beat.

2.
I am waiting for my shift to finish.
a buddy will pick me up
to go to a singles' bar downtown.
since I haven't received my uniform yet
I am wearing a sport's jacket
with the front left open
of course to show my gunbelt
and ease me through till midnight.

when we get to the bar I worry
what do I do with the gun?
I head to a solution in the men's room.
there I empty my gun,
tuck the bullets into my socks.
(I want gun and bullets to be apart)
gun belt and holster are rolled up
and stuffed into my jacket sleeve.

I carry the jacket back to our table,
roll up the coat and stuff it behind my back.
we order beer,
take turns asking girls to dance.
that way I know my gun is safe,
but I'm still
not my usual self
on the dance floor.

3.
part-time tailor is fixing my policeman's jacket.
on his desk, a photograph of three children.
those your kids? I ask.
sure are, he says.
how are they doing?
well, my daughter is in ballet
my sons are hockey players
all three are doing well in school.

after talking and making his kids bigger than life
he decides to say how he behaves
at company meetings:
I never say a word.
I always laugh or nod at precisely the right moments,
that way
people don't ask too many questions
and I've been working here for twenty years.

there is silence now.
he is still staring at the photograph.
what is going on in his eyes?
I clear my throat like I think I'm supposed to.
those aren't really my children, he says.
I bought that picture in a store.
just wanna be like the other guys
you know,
it's easier that way.

4.
in my uniform for the first time
I try to ride city transit for free
just like the city cops do
but I get caught when the bus driver
reminds me I'm not a city cop
and the wool of my baggy pants
makes me think
I'll end up paying
for this job.

5.
on the waterfront, sergeant barks:
your gun should only be loaded on the job
just before your shift begins.
I tell him I was only trying to be efficient
by loading the gun at home.
I never know why I do it though.
as I begin my shift at shed 10
a longshoreman and his wife speed
past me as if all C.P.R. cops are only there
to load their guns on time
and light up the cement
for the rats.

6.
seven a.m. on the docks again.
I see a floating hotel from France
docking the hugeness of its steel.
a woman, dressed to the sunrise in money,
descends for her day on the morning ramp
while leftover fog prepares her
for what's to come.
sure enough a longshoreman punches the day
with comments about her being
in the oldest profession.
a man she's with smacks the longshoreman so hard
he spins like a yo-yo into the river.
when I try to intervene like a good cop might
she tells me he's not worth it
and she's the one making
an honest living.

7.
out at Seagram's I'm like a watchman again
checking boxcar seals
to make sure booze is safe.
suddenly I hear a noise
and
another.
the sweat beneath my wool pants is too much.
night then lets loose a ragged set,
a ragged set of vocal chords:
it's only Sergeant Sirois, son,
just checking to make sure
you're on your toes.
C.P.R. policemen should always
be on their toes
RIGHT, son?

8.
on my beat at C.P. Express a driver motions to me
to get outside, fast.
there I see a man pulling a woman by her arm
across the C.P.R. parking lot.
I figure I should do something.
first, I yell: STOP.
then I blow my whistle.
next I flash my flashlight,
you know,
like they do on television.
I finally have to run up to them and say: HOLD IT.
that works.
he tells me he's taking his drunken wife home.
she says it's not true
and pulls up her skirt
showing bruise-covered thighs.
he beat me up outside a bar, she says.
what am I supposed to do, asks a voice?
believe it or not I'm able to flag down
a city police cruiser.
it works.
since I'm no longer on C.P.R. property
it's over.
I walk back across to the C.P.R. parking lot
and I don't know how to laugh
at being afraid
of my own fears.

Trust Company Messenger Boys

retired C.P.R. policemen carry messages
shuffling with lantern eyes
still watching their steps
over too many railroad ties.

Sam, the head messenger, points at Mort
and warns me to stay away from taverns
when I meet Mort between messages.

next day, as the sun just finishes
licking skyscrapers, I meet Mort.
sure enough we squint into a tavern
for glasses of messenger blues.

when we return an hour later
Sam blows us back to sober
with the ethics of messages.
Mort especially is yelled at
for helping me buzz away my job.

Mort pleads it was all his fault.
he was breaking me in
and blame is not so easy
for keeping the mail waiting.

And Then In The Briefcase

on the train going back East
a woman carries an oversized briefcase.
she brings it tó each meal
sits it on an empty chair beside her
even orders it a meal,
(a half grapefruit, please).

sometimes she speaks to herself,
occasionally to the briefcase,
and often to the night
beyond the window of her table.

three months earlier she and her husband
had planned a Vancouver trip
but he died two weeks before they went.
we'll go anyway, she had told herself.

so she had her man cremated,
his ashes placed in a container
and then in the briefcase.

at this moment she is angry with the dark.
the grapefruit is starting to frown at her.
she is asking me why the night
always lies about its age.

Occasionally Behind His Smoke

workers in this office call him
Bulldog behind his back.
he only looks like one sometimes.
beneath his corrugated face is really
a twenty-seven-year-old timid accountant.

when he asks me to do a job
he does it so carefully
you'd swear he teaches roses
how to be roses.
people say he has no accounts payable
but lots of accounts receivable.

as he tells a joke he laughs
like a boy unwrapping sex for the first time.
even his face becomes more dog-like
and the more sex jokes zoom across the lunchroom
the harder he puffs on his pipe
as if in back of his smoke
is a face on fire.

Polish The Cement

headshipper still has the same frown
he was born with.
he loves to lose his temper
as if it were part of his job.
I think he gets overtime for his rage.
if we're not busy when he walks by
we pretend to polish the floor
with leftover anxiety
from his last explosion.
if only his face could change its color?
yes, he wears grey pants, grey shirts
everything about him is grey.
I once dreamed about teaching his clothes
how to smile on their own.
he wouldn't,
he just wouldn't allow it.

Brown And Red

whenever comptroller feels nervous
he fingers his glasses up closer to his face.
always he is dressed in a dark brown suit,
white shirt and red tie.
he loves to be predictable in the office.

he reminds everyone each day he smokes
only one cigarette per day and just at lunchtime.
without exception he borrows one smoke from the same secretary.
he reminds her he's keeping count
and he expects us all to laugh at that joke.
I can't laugh on his cues.
that's why I'm an office boy.

I told him today I liked his taste in neckties.
he enjoyed that.
it took the pressure off me.

The Same Puddle

in the warehouse yard the other laborer
speaks of hide-a-bed burdens
as he stares so tired at cartoon trucks
in an after-the-rain-puddle.

warehouse boss
sensing the laborer's escape
snaps at him
a blue streak of his own:
GET THAT FURNITURE UNLOADED.

the laborer dips behind his own stare
and in order to quench his thirsty sublimation,
scoops water from his puddle
before getting back to work again.

spitting with company time disgust
into the same puddle
the boss proclaims:
you helpers will always be helpers,
you just can't
keep your drinking habits
away from the job.

When The Customer Is Calm

I am packing her china.
she is in the room attending to her child.
I want to enter the room and ask her
if she has any more breakables to pack.
after I knock she invites me in:
come on in, I'm only breast-feeding my baby.
do you have any more breakables, I ask.
in the closet, she says.
I try not looking at her breast
but the nipple is making me nervous.
customer knows it too.
she is becoming more relaxed
just to make me feel better, I'm sure.
her dripping breast has no effect on her.
are you afraid, she asks, her voice
like the tissue I use to wrap china.
she is now so tranquil.
I want to leap out of my skin
but the infant is not mine
and it is crying for more milk.

Leftover Booze And The Rabbi

his eyes say he likes to talk.
so do I but today I am no voice
for him.

in his house I'm wrapping his glasses.
he asks why I'm doing this job.
to make money, I say.
to do what? he asks.
maybe go back to school.
but what will happen when you can't buy knowledge at school?
do you want these nearly empty liquor bottles packed? I ask.
take them home, he says.
he is making me pay for more of his questions.
gotta get on with my job, I say.
I want to pack.
I want to pack his questions away
by wrapping a lamp's torso
in slow
slow motion
until the last carton has only room
for me.

Big Strong Boy True Story

while hauling furniture I often hear
other helpers joking
about getting seduced
by woman customers
on the job
but everyone agrees it never happens.

one day I am on a small pack and load job
with two other helpers.
I am in the master bedroom
packing personal items from anywhere
when in walks that woman.
you look like a big strong boy, she says.
in the next minute I hear big strong boy twice more
and then it happens.
I come across a condom box.
as I'm ready to pack it
into a carton
woman says: keep those
you've done a good job today.

as we're heading back, I pull out my gift
and show it to my co-workers.
well, the truck just rocks with laughter
the more,
the more I try,
the more I try to say it's true.

White Man

he laughs a lot
especially when someone calls him White Man.
he looks like he was born in white coveralls
in this warehouse.
whenever he speaks of sex
he pulls in his belly
like the day he tells my face
I need more sex
to clean my chin of pimples.

today White Man is telling a good story:
last night I was in bed
with two women.
both wanted to do it at the same time.
I was still half asleep of course.
well, at exactly the same time
they rolled on top of me
knocking their heads together.
helluva thing.
both got up to leave.
imagine, there I was
with the highest tent on my lap
you ever did see.

we all laughed at White Man's words.
it's not often he'll be so fluid.
you have to get him on a good day.

Dispatcher Sawdust

it's true.
dispatcher sounds like his voice is cutting wood.
he grinds out orders as if at any moment
someone will pull the plug on him.
he is a very efficient vice-president.
if only his speech would tell him so.

today I am printing numbers and letters
on a trailer when he comes out into the yard.
as he begins to speak a shouting contest explodes
from inside the warehouse.
gotta go, sounds like trouble, he says.

in the crate-making area I hear
the head warehouseman giving a blast
to a helper for being slow.
dispatcher tells both men
he'll now take over.

carefully,
ever so carefully he begins
to cut lumber for his idea of a crate.
I ask myself if he's using his vocal chords
to fashion the crate.
instead he uses his nerves.
they are that sharp.

Wallet

it hangs by its throat
on a chain
on his belt,
folded into its stomach
the thick of a dollar bill wad.

as a driver for this moving company
he's always looking for deals
from clients who have to move.

often he comes back to the warehouse
with a bureau or television,
today he has an empty wallet
and a face beyond happy,
what do you have in the truck? I ask.
Playboy Magazines, every issue to ever come out.
what are you going to do with them?
they're collectors' items, KID,
I can get a fortune for these.

days and days go by and not one buyer,
guys only ask to borrow them for the night.
soon the wallet becomes too hardened
and its owner is cursing the links
of his private lifeline.

Thoroughness Of My Nails And Wood

warehouse boss often rivets his bluntness
at my overseas crate-making.

out of kindness to my craft
I one day decide to seek out his expertise
for a motorcycle crate by having him place his hand
inside the crate to hold the gas tank
as I hammer
and for the first time he smiles
at the thoroughness of my nails and wood.

as I'm finishing he says he sees himself
riding the crate overseas
boasting of his success
in leading me on to perfection.

then he tells me his hand is stuck.
I'm tempted
to leave him there
but there is danger
in the way he imagines.

Bus Home From The Warehouse

in crowded hollows of a bus
widows clothed in daily black
hang their fatigue on steel bars.
the odour, more than anything else,
smells real.

men snooze on elbows and lunch buckets
except for one who sleeps open-eyed
with his manhood protruding
from a tear in old pants.

everyone is too tired to gasp or laugh
and
only lift glances in relief
at recognition of a bus stop.

as the wide-eyed sleeper prepares to exit
bus driver reminds him
he owes another fare
for his friend.

In The Calgary Eye Of A Montreal Night

while subway ignores dusk
billboard eyes glance hideously
at those of us who sell
more than jeans or cigarettes.

in a St. Catherine Street bar bodies angle
in sweat.
an announcer says:
for five bucks a song
a super sexy girl
will dance at your table.
more than one consecutive dance
with the same girl
make a deal with her.
the more you show her
the more she'll show you.
dancers cannot sit or drink
or linger at your table.
most important, do not touch your dancer
with anything except
another five dollar bill.

on my way home cathedrals become strippers
wearing Halloween masks
and their dances trick me
with strip joint blues
right into shopping bags
filled with billboards
and G-strings.

Cat-Face Story

by the table, a man stands with his new woman.
but before they can sit
his landlady tears off her brassiere,
places it on the table
for the sake of her comfort only.
after loosening her belt, she hoists her blouse
to show his new mate
the presence of surgical etchings.
in the casualness of four-letter feeling
she reminds his woman
you ain't good enough for him
if you can't read
the cat-face story on my belly.
glancing from the landlady's scars
to the brassiere and back again
the new mate replies: why
do you need a cat-face to speak for you?
I'll bet that animal
doesn't know why it's there.
right now the man just thinks
of telling them both
that the cat belongs in a book
where every second page rhymes
like the bell of another round
in a boxing match
between strangers.

As My Mother Tells It

as my mother tells it
she's on a plane from Calgary to Montreal
sitting next to a woman who used to cook
for an all-male crew.
the woman lets go with bush stories
buying my mother drinks ice-cubed
with four-lettered words
and mom tightens her dignity
saying it's because of air pockets.

the stories are of bushmen
straddling their paychecks
in an after-hour shack,
how they awake the next day
chasing poker chips
like maniac suns in the dawn.
when everything is gone
the men sell size twelve work boots
to that size ten winner.
my mother says that neither her
nor my father ever worked in isolation.

but she tells my mother she's smarter.
she's saved all her cash
for broadcasting school in Montreal
where she swears she'll try to unify
the sanity of her listeners.

In the Middle Of Stampede

you are not going to believe me
but it's two a.m. and I find myself shadow
to shadow with a woman
not a block from a nearly sleeping hotel.
are you a cop? she asks.
of course not, I laugh.
she says: it's not easy being what I am
in the middle of Stampede
but I charge between fifty and sixty.
moments later as my pockets show empty
an undercover cop snickers loudly
asking if I'm being solicited.
I tell him she's an old friend
and we're off for some coffee.
my pockets were only trying
to say it's her treat.
he walks too long with us
telling how he'd love to make it
with all those women in town for Stampede
and of course
he'd get it for nothing.
but I tell him in my head
he's just paid a very high price
for a few words
about his line in life.

Beneath The Tracks

Sarcee woman has no choice
but to stagger
to the middle of nobody's tunnel
where in the semi-dark
of carbon monoxide
she disgorges her past
in the presence of her dignity
only.

On Special Today

Chinese shop is invaded
by the open purse of a woman
carrying her husband
as a fading Peking lantern.

tell me.
does this have endurance?
is
that guaranteed?

each souvenir is smudged
till finally she hoards
a petrified donkey of wood.

the shop's owner reminds her
when the ass was placed on earth
it was given
a very thick skin.

Jessie's Boarding House

Jessie's only boarder,
her ex-husband,
sleeps on girlie magazines,
plays solitaire all day
down near Jessie's furnace.

her current husband living upstairs
cooks supper while Jessie works
twelve-hour shifts
behind a tavern snack food bar.

the two men eat together,
play chess,
and
pretend to not take the game
too seriously.
neither seems to ever win.
they are both too happy
to be brilliant.

Making Me Behave

so you won't buy a ticket to your own funeral?
but you are nearly there, you know.
the closer you get the more genial you become.
did you once say you didn't want to be
a bad actor in a good movie?
you're almost arrogant
about the new head of hair you'll have
when the treatments stop
but I know you're acting like the performer
you wish you were.
there's an idea in my head making me behave
like an actor with only one star
beside his picture.
the idea shows you trying
to close the door
in your dressing room
and the music,
yes, the idea's music
is beginning to question my behavior.

Ice Time

cutting across a park in late November
I stop,
hear voices coming from the bottom
of an empty swimming pool.
a group of boys are playing hockey
with the yellow of a tennis ball.
I don't disturb them.
imagine, playing ball hockey
on the floor of an autumn pool.
the boys are warming up
taking shots from the shallow end
to the deep end.
goaltender finds it easier that way
and
he is using school bags for goalposts.
now that makes sense.
he is letting his friends learn
to put homework
where it should be,
in the middle
of an almost November dark.

Rocky Eyes

Eye 1.
mountain goat at a roadside
paws his profile into focus.
he knows his best angle.
in his sleep he postcard-poses.

Eye 2.
water drips from stone pores
like overanxious sweat
on a hiker's neck.

Eye 3.
hypnotized snow snakes
awakened by clouds
snap their fingers
to the beat
of your song.

Eye 4.
mountainside has a rash
on its ridge.
all that's left from fire.

As The Snow Arms Melted

I drive through the black mountains
weaving to fixed positions
but at different angles to the earth
as if I were competing
with the contortions of snow.

I look,
I look out from my car
into that crossword game of sky.
mountains are ink blotters standing face-up.
Spring is pretending to be there in the night.

ballpoint nibs posing as insects
scribble their lives
on the wings of giant ravens.
before too long these insects
find the white of themselves
splashing onto my windshield.

a deer on the highway stands rigid
in its skin
as if to intrude on my nightdreaming.
I brake hard,
roll down my window,
beg forgiveness from the deer
but
I can't avoid the moth
slamming to its death on my left temple.

trotting across the highway
the deer eyes me with a warning:
next time
insects won't die so easily
and every imagination
won't keep up with the shape of snow.

Pulling The Sunset Tighter

can you hear that groaning?
sky is wounded from an arrowhead
nearly buried in cloud.
in a farmer's field nearby
hay bales are becoming
flocks of animals scared awake
by sheet lightning.
both horizon and field
want a story read to them
to calm their differences.

man beside me speaks of finding
twenty-six arrowheads
at the bottom of a buffalo jump.
must've missed one, he says,
pointing to where horizon and field
are becoming impatient.

I am waiting for the rest of his story.
I want to hear about that bow
of cloud across sky
and
how it is pulling the sunset
tighter and tighter as its string.

Maybe The Music

I am listening to the sounds
of the ceiling F.M. music
coaxing the day from the floor.
two window washers ignore their own images
as they get a start on shoe store glass.
still all ears I walk into another store
wanting to break the morning quiet
by buying the print of A.M. news.
cashier is counting last night's returns.
three stacks of bills reach up like speakers.
I listen to the sounds of the growing money walls.
in the mall there is the beginning of rock music.
maybe ceiling songs don't know
how to look for pure anymore.
but maybe #2 says:
the music is like a salesman
selling himself a bargain lie.

On The Lap Of A Spring Sea, My Woman

on most nights I'm about as easy to read
as those endless pages of Alberta sky.
secrets are resting in corners.
piled like shrunken glaciers
on the lap of a Spring sea,
but (she knows).

when evening sky is easier to read
humanity sirens are mute.
with my ear to the ground, I hear oceans
diluting eons of earth dregs
and (her silence is writing this poem).

in a half dream last night
I heard a man laughing loudly.
he gave me his sponge to soak up trickles
posing as tidal waves
but (she has long since decoded
the sky's own alphabet —
she is speaking this poem for me).

Soft Monologue

he is looking for his father:
in a glass so heavy
it cannot be lifted,
in his sister's music box
where musicians look
upon fatigue like disease
but he finds him only
in the picture that fills
the song of his private self.
in that picture
he is following his father
to the accused box at a trial —
nothing sentimental, mind you,
but he is saying DADDY over
and over again
but his father says: you,
you wouldn't want to come
into the bucket with me
would you?
he finally decides to stop
the breathing of his picture
and listen to the light tapping
of an ever-smiling conductor.

First Chapter Of Its Blood

I can't understand the prairie today.
too many are borrowing from its speech
till they don't even know
whose language they are speaking.

documents are being re-written
to duplicate someone's realism
as if the weak artist were stealing
and the strong artist were imitating.

the land just wants to lie down,
listen to the first chapter of its blood
learning how to speak again.
only the rain will allow any direction
to squeeze itself from soil.

the prairie's semblance of code
comes from the mud of centuries.
the product belongs only to the coyote
and the coyote who waits will die
without having said a word.

My Sleep Like The City

my sleep like the city is slowly,
slowly losing its grey.
buildings stand questioning
each other under mist.
they are trying to start the day.
the bridge is a set of dentures,
the bridge is speaking my dream —
I'm being chased by religious zealots
from a cult with no name.
first, I'm driving a red truck,
then, I'm on a bicycle
which I carefully hide
beneath the front steps of a seminary.
finally, I'm on foot.
as long as I keep,
as long as I keep walking
I never get caught.
when I awake I wish
I were a Portuguese rooster
practicing my cry for a half-hour
before announcing the sun.